better together*

*This book is best read together, grownup and kid.

 akidsco.com

a
kids
book
about

a kids book about

adopting
a pet

the dodo

a kids book about

A Kids Book About books are available online: *akidsco.com*

To share your stories, ask questions, or inquire about bulk
purchases (schools, libraries, and nonprofits), please use
the following email address: *hello@akidsco.com*

ISBN: 978-1-953955-86-9

Designed by Duke Stebbins and Gabby Nguyen
Edited by Emma Wolf

This book is for all the pets
out there who are waiting patiently
for their loving families.

Intro

At some point, kids will probably ask their grownups for a pet. But they may not have a lot of information about the different ways you can go about finding a pet. This book explains the process of adopting a pet from a shelter or a rescue and why it's an amazing thing to do—for the pet who finally gets their own family, and the adopters who experience the joy of welcoming an animal who needs them into their lives.

Teaching kids about pet adoption will encourage them to play a more active role in selecting a pet, and, more importantly, to develop empathy. Rescue pets teach all of us, kids and grownups alike, to think more deeply about how to care for others, understand what they've been through, and learn what we can do to create a comfortable and happy environment for them to thrive.

We're going to start
this book off with some
good news...

and some bad news.

First, the

bad news...

there are pets out there
who don't have homes.

But here's the

good news:

you can give one of these pets
the best gift ever—a loving home.

How?

Pet adoption.
That's right!

People like you and me can help pets who don't have families find safe, loving, and caring homes.

Adopting a pet is when you find your new best friend and welcome them into your family!

Pets who need to be adopted usually live at an animal shelter or rescue group.

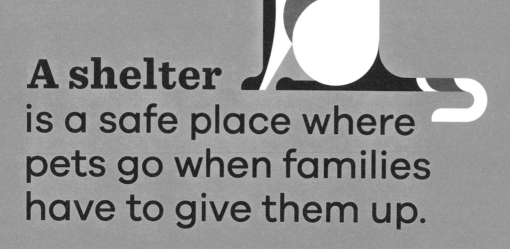

A shelter is a safe place where pets go when families have to give them up.

People who work there take care of animals and can help your family find a friend who's the right match for you.

An animal rescue is a group that takes care of animals when shelters are too full to keep them.

They also remove animals from unhealthy situations, place them in foster homes, and help them find new families who will love them forever.

And this is true for animals of ALL kinds!

Just like there are so many different kinds of people... there are SO many kinds of animals who need to be adopted.

Young ones.

Old ones.

Small ones.

Big ones.

Fluffy ones.

Not-so-fluffy ones.

So, **why** should you adopt a pet?

This one is easy...

because it's amazing!

You get a new member of your family, and you get...

- to help an animal in need,

- someone who will love you unconditionally,

- someone to snuggle with,

- someone who does a happy dance when you come home,

- and someone who thinks you're the very best thing that's ever happened to them.

That all sounds
pretty great, right?

So maybe you're
asking yourself...

how

can I adopt a pet?

1

Well, the first step is
to talk to your grownups.

Chat about what kind of pet
would be happiest in your family.

Do you want to take several long walks a day, in all kinds of weather?

Or would a couch potato pet be a better fit?

What are the qualities that are most important to you, and what other questions do you have about pets?

If you have a friend who has adopted a pet, you can ask them about the shelter or rescue group they got their pet from.

You can continue your search online, which is something your grownups can help with!

You can also visit your local shelter and talk to the people who are caring for the animals.

They can help you with your search!

You can find out lots of important things about animals who need homes, like:

if they do well with kids,

how they respond to loud noises,

or if they have any
health conditions you
may need to consider
before taking them home.

Once you've found the pet that's perfect for your family, it's time to know if you and your family are the right fit for them too!

You might fill out an application, spend some time together, or talk about yourself and your family with someone at the shelter or rescue.

And once all of that is done, you get to welcome your pet into their new family!

They're officially yours,
to take care of and to

love.

But that's not the end...
it's just the beginning.

Once you get home... remember that everything is new for you and your pet, and it might take time to feel at home.

Think about when you go to a new school or join a new team— it's not always easy right away.

It can take time to get used to things and feel comfortable.

It's a lot like that for your new pet!

And while your pet is getting comfortable, know it's also going to take time for you to understand your pet.

Adopted pets come from many different backgrounds.

The best thing you can do is watch and listen closely to learn what they're feeling and what they need.

Do they get shy or overwhelmed in certain situations?

Do they love it when you scratch them behind their ears?

Where do they go when they want to relax?

You're on your way
to becoming the
expert
on your pet!

Some people think if your adopted pet isn't relaxed and calm right away, you should take them back to the shelter.

But that's not true.

Your new pet is going through a LOT of changes.

And just like people, animals may not act like themselves when they're confused or scared.

Think about how you
would feel if, all of a sudden,
you had a whole new family,
home, and rhythm to your life!

It might take a few weeks for a pet to feel safe enough to show their real personality and start goofing around.

Here are a few fun ways to get to know your new pet:

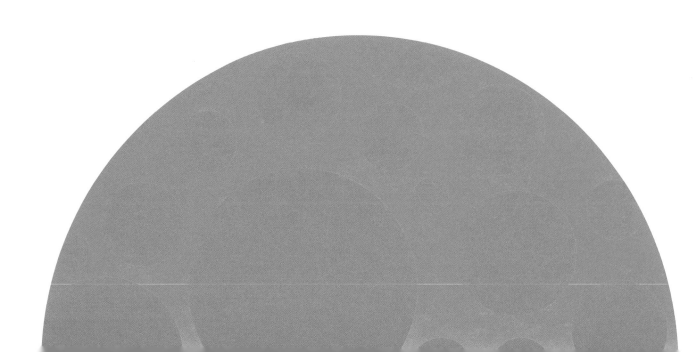

- Encourage your pet to take an official tour of their new home.

- Get some exercise together.

- Sit quietly, not doing anything!

There will be lots of firsts with your new pet, like...

- the first time they come when you call their name,

- the first time they lie down next to you to cuddle,

- and the first time they comfort you when you're having a bad day.

And the excitement doesn't end with the "firsts."

There are so many things to come, like...

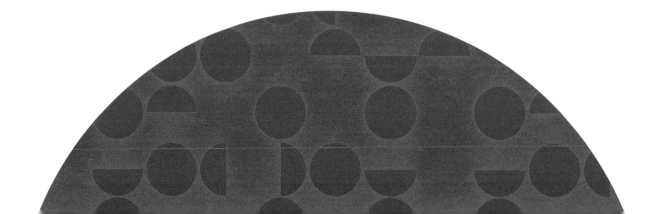

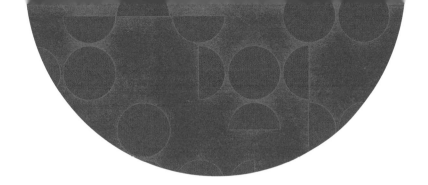

- celebrating their birthday or adoptaversary,*

- discovering their favorite foods,

- or seeing them learn amazing tricks.

And especially, growing up together.

*The day you adopted them!

Your new pet is a family member—one who will give you unconditional love and endless FUN.

You are your pet's favorite person in the whole world.

Your pet now has a

loving

and fa

home

mily...

because

of you.

Outro

We hope we've explained pet adoption in a way that resonates with your kid, and that we've helped them understand the pet adoption process and why it's a great option.

We also hope the information provided in this book about shelters and rescues builds confidence in how to go about adopting a pet, and how to be mindful and prepared when choosing a pet to bring home.

Most of all, we hope it inspires everyone to think about what it means to welcome an animal into their family—and how uniquely special it is to adopt a pet who needs a place to call home.

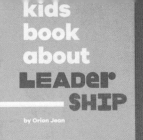

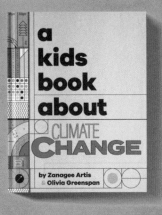
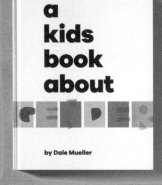

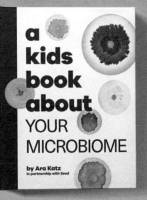